OPERATION
Nineveh

OPERATION
Nineveh

39 DAYS
WITH JONAH

BROTHER ANDREW
WITH AL JANSSEN

INTRODUCTION

*J*onah had a problem. He couldn't in good conscience obey God's command.

To understand Jonah's struggle, it might help to frame his mission in a contemporary context. "Jonah, arise and go to Baghdad. Go to Al Qaeda and preach against them, because their wickedness has come up before me."

God told Jonah to go to Nineveh, which was located in what today is northern Iraq, within the suburbs of modern-day Mosul. The Assyrians who lived in that great city were the most feared terrorists of that day. And they hated Israel. Put it that way and perhaps we gain some sympathy for Jonah. We might have run away from that assignment too.

Over the next few weeks as we study this short book we will see just how relevant this drama is to the current world situation. Like Jonah, God has issued a call on our lives. Are we listening? Are we willing to go wherever He sends us in obedience? Or are we going to run away and take a Mediterranean cruise instead?

Thirty-nine days is a long time. We like quick solutions. Why not cover this in three days? Or perhaps a single Sunday morning sermon? We prefer short-term missions rather than a long-time commitment. Better yet, we prefer to do missions from a safe distance. We prefer the use of smart bombs that can reach any target—except the hearts and minds of men. But it's hearts and minds we must touch if we're to have any chance of winning this spiritual battle.

Now, I need to warn you—this study is dangerous. I believe the book of Jonah offers radical solutions to today's problems. I'm talking about the threat of terrorism, the challenge of Muslim extremism, even the cultural shifts occurring with immigrants from Islamic countries. You may not like everything you read. You'll probably disagree at times. But I hope you won't toss these words aside in frustration. Instead think about them and pray.

This study of Jonah is full of questions that challenge me. I hope they will challenge you as well. I admit that I have more questions than answers. Questions that force me, force us, to make some choices.

The consequence of our choices could affect the future of our world.

What do you hope to gain from this devotional in the next 39 days?

DAY ONE

"The word of the LORD came to Jonah son of Amittai" (Jonah 1:1).

*O*peration Nineveh starts with: "The Word of the LORD came to Jonah."

How did Jonah receive this Word?

It might have started on a cool evening sometime between 780 and 750 B.C. while Jonah relaxed on his back patio. For this prophet life was good. Other prophets railed against the people and proclaimed God's judgment. They were persecuted and even killed because their messages were so unpopular. (That's what Jesus said in Luke 11:47-48.) But Jonah was popular with the people and the political establishment. His message to King Jeroboam II was that God would restore the lost borders of Israel (2 Kings 14:25). Finally some good news after so many defeats! And then to see his prophecy fulfilled. He was welcome anytime in the king's court.

"Jonah!" the voice called. Probably one of his neighbors or a cousin, he thought. Couldn't they leave him alone at the end of a long, hot day? But the rules of hospitality required that you never leave your neighbor standing outside, not even in the middle of the night. Who knows? Maybe he had some unexpected guests who needed bread.

"Come in," Jonah answered.

"Jonah!"

Oh no! That was neither his neighbor, nor his cousin. This was his Boss! He'd better get out of his chair and answer.

"Yes Lord."

Of course he knew when the Lord started speaking; he was a prophet after all. There were not many prophets in Jonah's time. Actually, it seemed God did not speak much anymore and it surely showed in the life of the nation. Despite recent military gains, there were enemies inside and outside Israel's borders. Whether you looked at things from an economic, moral or spiritual perspective, there was little cause for rejoicing.

The name "Jonah" means "dove" which is the symbol of the Holy Spirit who searches the very depth of our hearts. Jonah's job as a prophet was to submit to the Holy Spirit. However, as we'll soon see, Jonah instead argued with God.

How do we respond when we hear the Word of the Lord? A Russian pastor, during the years when Bibles were not allowed to be printed in the Soviet Union, in answer to prayer received a copy of the Bible and eagerly distributed pages to each person in his church. The next day the pastor was in town and saw a member of his congregation with a big smile. "You must have gotten a good page," said the pastor. "Oh yes," said the man. "I received a page from Jeremiah!" "Oh, that gloomy prophet," said the pastor. "He preached his heart out and never saw any results. I have a page from Matthew. Why don't we swap?" The man said, "Oh no pastor. Listen to what this says. 'The Word of the LORD came to Jeremiah.' If the Word of the Lord can come to Jeremiah, it can come to me too!"

God spoke to Jonah because Jonah had a relationship with God. God also speaks to us if we have a relationship with Him. Are we listening? Do we hear Him? Are we eager to receive God's Word? Are we ready to obey it?

Or are our heads filled with noise? Are the headphones of an MP3 player constantly plugged into our ears? Must we always have the television on in the room? Are our schedules filled to overflowing with meetings and activities? If so, how do we know when God is speaking to us?

What are the consequences if we miss God's Word to us? They could be catastrophic—eternity may hang in the balance for millions of souls.

Can you hear God's voice in your life, or is there too much outside noise? How do you recognize God's voice?

_____

_____

_____

_____

_____

_____

_____

_____

_____

_____

_____

_____

_____

_____

_____

_____

DAY TWO

*"Go to the great city of Nineveh and preach against it,
because its wickedness has come up before me" (Jonah 1:2).*

Try to understand Jonah's problem: He had to go to the enemies of his people. The Assyrians were making forays into northern Israel where Jonah lived. It's entirely possible that they had attacked his home village of Gath-hepher. Perhaps Assyrians had killed his mother and father. Or maybe he had watched soldiers rape his sisters. If that's the case, we can certainly understand why Jonah hated this assignment. Being told to go to Nineveh would be like being ordered today to go to Baghdad.

However, Jonah should also have been pleased to learn that the wickedness of Nineveh had come to God's attention. Jonah believed the Assyrians should be judged for their brutality. Jonah's solution: Go...and kill them!

But God has a different message. Go...and WIN them.

You have to be divine to make friends with your enemies.

We don't live in a friendly environment. I certainly don't in Holland. There is plenty of bad news in the papers each day. There is a lot of anti-Christian sentiment throughout the country. And though I live in a town with many churches, there are also several mosques. On Friday afternoons, in my office, I often hear the loudspeaker from the nearby mosque.

When I go shopping at the Saturday market, there are numerous Muslim families in the crowd—you can easily recognize them by the way the men walk and because the women wear headscarves.

What do they think of Christians? Are they being greeted by us with a smile and a hearty "Good morning"?

Recently a Muslim man walked his bicycle past my home. I saw he had a flat tire so I stopped him and asked if I could help. It turned out that he had seven punctures in one of his tires. I invited him in, served him coffee, and fixed his tire.

If we don't start the process of making friends in a relatively friendly environment, how can we expect to do it in a hostile environment?

Are there Muslims living in your neighborhood? How are you praying for them? How might you reach out and befriend one of them?

DAY THREE

"But Jonah ran away from the LORD and headed for Tarshish. He went down to Joppa, where he found a ship bound for that port. After paying the fare, he went aboard and sailed for Tarshish to flee from the LORD" (Jonah 1:3).

*I*t is easier to identify with Jonah than with any other prophet. Others are so holy. Jonah is so much like us.

God says: Go ye!

Jonah says: No!

Jonah's basic problem: he had too much love for himself. He thought: "God will make a fool of me. I'll lose face."

He refused to be a fool for Christ.

He wanted God, but not God's kingdom. He wanted blessing without responsibility.

He was not making people ripe for hell. He just let them go to hell. He had no compassion for the lost.

What he did have was money. So rather than going east to Iraq, he headed west and bought a ticket for a Mediterranean cruise. He figured it was his money and he could spend it any way he chose. He didn't stop to think that he was spending God's money. Jonah pays with God's money to escape from God's call.

There is a burden on us. It's called the Great Commission. Go into all the world and make disciples of all nations (Matthew 28:19a). I believe God has called enough people in each generation to fulfill the Great Commission in their lifetime. But too many have run away.

Where is our compassion? God is not willing that ANY should perish! That applies to Nineveh and Amsterdam and New York. WE are responsible for the Ninevehs of this world.

Why do we not weep for Muslims? Yes, why don't we weep for fundamentalists?

Is it because we'd rather be entertained?

A man must be either entertained or challenged. It costs all your money to be entertained: television, radio, literature, cruises, time share condominiums, sport, travel (that includes the Holy Land), luxuries, food, eating out… (plus all at the expense of "family life.") And then, we've LOST all, everything.

We put so much on credit that there's nothing left for God's work. We borrow for "things." Do we ever borrow for missions? We cannot give what we do not have, and "to have" is *un*scriptural—the verb "to have" is not in the Hebrew language. However "to be" is; it is even God's name.

It costs nothing to be challenged—only your life.

We're stewards.

All that we have is entrusted to us.

And one day we must give an account (Romans 14:12).

Jonah ran because he saw opportunities as an enemy instead of the enemy as his biggest opportunity.

Do you have compassion for the lost? If so, what are you doing with it? If not, why not?

_____

_____

_____

_____

_____

_____

_____

_____

_____

_____

_____

_____

_____

_____

_____

_____

_____

DAY FOUR

⌒

*"Then the LORD sent a great wind on the sea, and such a
violent storm arose that the ship threatened to break up"
(Jonah 1:4).*

*J*onah boarded the ship and heaved a sigh of relief. He'd done
it! He ran away from God, and God didn't stop him. There
was no way he was going to those dreaded Assyrians in Nineveh. If
God wanted to send those terrorists a message, well He could find
someone else to deliver it.

Jonah stood on the bow and watched as the city of Joppa faded
into the distance. He loved the feeling of wind on his face. It was a
beautiful evening. The clouds were full of rich color as the sun set into
the Mediterranean Sea. He could smell dinner being prepared in the
galley. He would be eating at the captain's table. This was the life! Then
he turned his attention to the black clouds forming to the North. "I
think we're in for a storm," said one of the sailors behind him.

A pang of fear stabbed him. Was this the moment when Jonah
began to suspect that he was in trouble?

We can run from God, but we can't hide.

One of the messages clearly communicated throughout the
book of Jonah is God's sovereignty over nature.

"The LORD sent a great wind" (1:4).

"The LORD provided a great fish to swallow Jonah" (1:17).

"The LORD commanded the fish, and it vomited Jonah onto dry land" (2:10).

"God provided a vine and made it grow up over Jonah" (4:6).

"God provided a worm, which chewed the vine so that it withered" (4:7).

"God provided a scorching east wind" (4:8).

God has total control over nature. God's creation knows God's voice and obeys His commands. He spoke to the fish because the fish wouldn't argue with Him. Creation is God's tool to get Jonah back on the right track.

God didn't send a storm to pester Jonah but to save Nineveh.

Creation knows God's voice and obey His commands. Do you? How do you respond when God gives you a difficult assignment? Do you tend to ignore it? Run away? Or willingly obey?

_____

_____

_____

_____

_____

_____

_____

_____

_____

_____

_____

_____

_____

_____

_____

_____

_____

_____

DAY FIVE

⌢

*"All the sailors were afraid and each cried out to his
own god. And they threw the cargo into the sea to
lighten the ship. But Jonah had gone below deck, where
he lay down and fell into a deep sleep" (Jonah 1:5).*

*T*oo many people make up in speed for what they lack in
direction!

Jonah was in the wrong location: he should have been walking
on solid ground in Nineveh rather than staggering on the rolling sea.
Jonah was with the wrong company: he should have been meeting
with Nineveh's sinners and seekers instead of cursing sailors.

Sure the sailors were religious—in times of crisis we all are! And
while they cried out to their gods and tried to save the ship, Jonah
slept. The sailors were so amazed that a man with such a bad conscience could sleep so well!

Jonah had a wrong theology: God cares for Jews only. He had
a wrong attitude toward Gentiles: Get lost! (Doing nothing or running away is the same as saying "Get lost.")

But God loves lost people and so He gives us a second chance.
Yes, that's true today. God has not written off the world. Or you. Or
the person you are going to meet in your "Nineveh."

Question: Hasn't the world passed the point of "no return"?

I don't believe that. There is still hope. God can still change a city, a society, a nation. What will it take for us to wake up and realize that *now* is the time for us to announce God's solution to a desperate world? Must we first endure a few more horrific terrorist attacks—is that what is necessary to wake us up?

Answer: Who knows? (Jonah 3:9) God knows and He's calling *you*. You may *not* know the answers. But you can know God—His character, His love. And that's enough, provided you recognize His voice.

Most Christians do not know God. They sit east of the city (Jonah 4:5a) to watch the sun set on a sinful world, to watch cultures destroyed and peoples lost. They just sit and watch it on TV.

That's Spectator Christianity.

> *"It's terrible to be in chains*
> *To die in captivity.*
> *But it's worse to sleep, to sleep, to sleep in liberty."*

(A poem shared throughout Czechoslovakia during Communism that is based on Taras Shevchenko's *"The Days Go By".*)

Are you living life as if the world has passed the point of no return? Or are you looking for opportunities in which you can contribute to the solution? What is one opportunity where you can make a difference?

_____

_____

_____

_____

_____

_____

_____

_____

_____

_____

_____

_____

DAY SIX

〜

"The captain went to him and said, 'How can you
sleep? Get up and call on your god! Maybe he will take
notice of us, and we will not perish'" (Jonah 1:6).

*T*he captain tried everything. He ordered the sailors to
lighten the load, so the cargo was thrown overboard. If they
survived the storm, they would lose all of the revenue from this trip.
Someone suggested that they pray. So all the sailors prayed to their
gods. But the storm grew only more intense.

The captain shouted over the howling wind, "I'm out of ideas.
Does anyone else have any suggestions?"

One of the men replied: "You know that crazy Hebrew we took
on board at Joppa? Well while we carried up the cargo from the
hold, I couldn't help noticing that he's sound asleep."

Someone else said, "Why isn't he praying?"

"I'll go find out," said the captain. Holding onto the railing, he
struggled to keep his footing as he made his way down the stairs to
Jonah's bed. Sure enough, the Hebrew was sound asleep. He was
snoring!

If nothing else will wake us up, maybe the LOST will wake us up!

Jonah ran away from God. The *heathen* sailors told Jonah to go
back to his God. Sounds strange, but the sailors challenged Jonah
because of their dire need.

Today it's the same. A few years ago I was speaking with Mahmoud Zahar, one of the founders and leaders of Hamas. I had challenged him to stop the suicide bombings in Israel because "Jesus is against violence." Mahmoud sadly shook his head and said, "But Andrew, Jesus is not here anymore."

I wanted to cry, "But I'm here! Don't you see Jesus in me?"

On another occasion a wonderful Palestinian professor of Islam lamented the state of his people and then pleaded with me: "Andrew, if you are still in touch with Jesus, will you ask Him to come soon and help us?" It was a sincere plea.

The captain likewise pleaded with Jonah.

Why did the sailors ask Jonah to call on his God? Because he *had* something that might meet their need. Jonah had told them that he was running away from God. Obviously he knew something about his God that the sailors did not know about their gods. The difference was that Jonah had a relationship with God. And if he had a relationship with God, maybe he could intercede on their behalf.

Do you hear the cry of the lost? They are telling us to wake up and give them hope. You protest: "They never ask me about my faith, not like the sailors asked Jonah." Perhaps, you aren't asked because you don't live a different life. No one is jealous of you. Nobody wants what you have. You are so neutral that you have not even offended anyone.

It's terrible to live and not know why you were born.

It's terrible to die and not know why you lived.

When was the last time someone asked you why you are different? Have they ever? Why or why not? Do you know what you would say if they ever asked?

_____

_____

_____

_____

_____

_____

_____

_____

_____

_____

_____

_____

_____

_____

_____

_____

_____

DAY SEVEN

*"Then the sailors said to each other,
'Come, let us cast lots to find out who is responsible for
this calamity.' They cast lots and the lot fell on Jonah.
So they asked him, 'Tell us, who is responsible for
making all this trouble for us? What do you do?
Where do you come from? What is your country?
From what people are you?'" (Jonah 1:7-8).*

Shouting over the noise of the wind, the sailors asked Jonah five questions. They weren't interested in Jonah's opinions or preferences or even his beliefs. They wanted to know his responsibility: "What do you do?" They wanted to know "What is your country?" and "From what people are you?" because they needed to determine who was Jonah's God.

Big question: What is our occupation? Our ministry? Our responsibility?

The world has a right to ask.

Jonah's responsibility was to his (nation's) enemies, to bring them a message that would save them based on a God who loves and forgives.

Our responsibility is: Matthew 28, the Great Commission. Go! Make disciples! Teach them all I (Jesus) have commanded.

As long as they ask, there is hope. But we have no right to be heard unless we first earn the right to their attention.

How would you answer the sailors' questions? That depends on how well you know God. You might be asleep to the need around you. But the world will wake you up and demand "What is your business?" That is what angry Muslims want to know. They demand, "Why you are afraid of us? What are you hiding from us?" Our crisis today is one of credibility.

There are few missionaries in the Muslim world—in fact in some countries missionaries and proclamation of the Gospel are prohibited. But Muslims still want to know. When the movie *Passion of the Christ* was released, it was shown in many Muslim countries and theaters were packed. In one large Muslim country, I saw DVDs of the movie for sale on the street for one dollar. Yes, they want to know!

But what is our calling card? When they look to the "Christian" West, they see our television shows and movies and rock stars. Is that our occupation—to send them the filth from our culture?

There's nothing wrong with Muslims physically, morally or mentally.

They lack one dimension: A future—hope, faith, security, forgiveness, eternal life.

You know the answer.

Go and give it!

How would you answer the sailors' questions? When the world asks will you be ready to answer?

DAY EIGHT

⁓

*"He answered, 'I am a Hebrew and I worship the
LORD, the God of heaven, who made the sea and the
land.' This terrified them and they asked, 'What have
you done?' (They knew he was running away from the
LORD, because he had already told them so.)" (Jonah
1:9-10).*

*D*on't ever become a runaway prophet. Actually, a "runaway
prophet" is an oxymoron, like a leader without any followers. When you admit you ran away from God, your first concern
should be to run back to Him. Otherwise you have no testimony left.
Therefore, you won't see results. We are not seeing the Great Commission fulfilled because too many of God's people are running away.

Only Christians who can look others in the eye are able to witness. The world demands: "What are you withholding from us that
we need to know?" Jonah's answer to the sailors is honest, but fee-
ble. There was no proclamation. He doesn't tell them how they can
know God—just how they can escape from their present peril.

Does the world see a difference in us? If not, they won't listen
to our message.

Nineveh's problem: they were lost and there was no one to show
them the way.

Jonah's problem: he knew too much of the way to enjoy running away.

Our problem: We're too Christian to enjoy sin, and too sinful to enjoy God. That's why we're so miserable.

The only cure: radical preaching and radical response.

There is no risk in following Jesus.

There is terrible risk in not following Jesus.

Are you withholding life-saving information from the lost? Why? What will it take for you to share it?

DAY NINE

*"The sea was getting rougher and rougher. So they
asked him, 'What should we do to you to make the sea
calm down for us?' 'Pick me up and throw me into the
sea,' he replied, 'and it will become calm. I know that
it is my fault that this great storm has come upon you.'"*
(Jonah 1:11-12).

Something has to happen; someone has to *die*.

There comes a point in time when God's patience is
exhausted. Then "grace" ends and "judgment" begins. This applies
to an individual and to a nation. Both are frequently described in
the Old Testament to teach us. Have we heeded?

When God's patience with Jonah is exhausted, Jonah becomes
the "ransom" by receiving God's judgment, thereby saving the lives
of the sailors.

In order for the sailors to live Jonah had to die. That much is
clear. So why didn't Jonah just jump into the sea? Maybe he wasn't
really willing to give up his life? Unless a grain of wheat falls into
the ground and dies, there is no harvest (John 12:24). Unless Jonah
falls into the sea and dies, there will be no salvation for the sailors.
Or for Nineveh.

Jesus said that in order to save your life, you have to lose it. But
Jonah is not going to commit suicide—that is never our call. The

27

Christian life is radically different from the call of Islam. We are never asked to blow ourselves up and take as many people as possible with us. Jonah knows he has to die, but he can not take his own life. Rather, he must offer up his life to save those of the sailors.

This is what I call sacramental living. We must offer up our lives. We do that by giving up our rights so that others, who do not know Jesus, may have the right to hear the good news of the Gospel.

Some may question the term "sacramental." I mean it in the sense that Paul explains in his letter to the Colossians: "I rejoice in what was suffered for you, and I fill up in my flesh what is still lacking in regard to Christ's afflictions, for the sake of his body, which is the church" (Colossians 1:24).

Jonah's words to the sailors: "Throw me into the sea." He was still a prophet. When he said the sea would become calm, he was speaking the truth. All that was needed was for him to die.

What rights are you holding onto that the Lord is asking you to give up?

DAY TEN

"Instead the men did their best to row back to land. But they could not, for the sea grew even wilder than before. Then they cried to the LORD, 'O LORD, please do not let us die for taking this man's life. Do not hold us accountable for killing an innocent man, for you, O LORD, have done as you pleased.'" (Jonah 1:13-14).

*W*hy didn't the sailors immediately follow Jonah's instructions? Instead they manned the oars and tried to row back to land. Come to think of it, why didn't they try rowing earlier? Probably because they knew such effort was futile.

The sailors showed more concern for one man than Jonah did for one million Ninevites.

Some think that only Christians are good people. That's not true. Those sailors were good people. They accepted responsibility for their passenger. They did everything possible to save Jonah. Just imagine them pulling on their oars with waves crashing over the boat. They couldn't even see land—how did they know which direction to row? Still they had to try.

There are many good non-Christians. There are many Muslims who are very good people. We don't enhance our witness by demonizing Muslims, by making them out to be our enemies, by believing that they are all radical fundamentalists who would force us to submit to their religion.

Here is another possibility. How many Muslims really want to know what Jesus has done for them? I wonder if the sailors didn't throw the man of God overboard because they knew they would lose all chance to learn more about this God who controls nature. However, the sea grew wilder. Finally, to save themselves, they had to throw Jonah overboard.

Was their last hope gone? The sailors must have had their doubts. They threw a paying passenger overboard and now they had no prophet, no message from God, no knowledge of what they must do to know God.

Would you know what to do if in your community there was no church, no Bible, no Christian neighbors?

DAY ELEVEN

*"Then they took Jonah and threw him overboard, and
the raging sea grew calm. At this the men greatly feared
the L*ORD*, and they offered a sacrifice to the L*ORD *and
made vows to him" (Jonah 1:15-16).*

*G*od says "I am the LORD." Meaning God can send a storm on
the sea, or in your life. And God can still the storm—on the
sea, and in your life.

Was Jonah's death the end or the beginning?

It was a beginning for the sailors—they worshiped the God of
creation and made vows to Him.

Does God listen to a prayer of a non-Christian?

Does God listen to a prayer from a church spire?

Does God listen to a prayer from a minaret?

The answer to all three questions is "Yes," because God hears a
cry from the heart.

First, the sailors prayed to their gods because Jonah didn't give
them reason to pray to His God. Then they rowed. Then they prayed
to Jonah's God. And a miracle occurred. As a result they sacrificed
to God. They made vows to God. What kind of vows? Probably like
the ones we make: Lord if you save me from this mess I will serve
you for the rest of my life.

Unfortunately we usually forget our vows when the problem is solved. But don't worry: God will remind you.

This was also the beginning of a new life for Jonah. Jesus said: "Unless a kernel of wheat falls to the ground and dies, it remains only a single seed. But if it dies, it produces many seeds" (John 12:24).

We all must die.

We must die to religion.

We must die to pride.

We must die to politics.

We must die to culture.

Only then can we begin again with real life in Christ.

Jonah is a type of Jesus—by voluntarily giving himself.

Jonah is also an anti-type of Jesus:

Jesus was innocent and crucified for the guilty.

Jonah was guilty and was thrown overboard to save the "innocent."

This is "sacramental" living.

"We always carry around in our body the death of Jesus, so that the life of Jesus may also be revealed in our body. For we who are alive are always being given over to death for Jesus' sake, so that his life may also be revealed in our mortal body. So then, death is at work in us, but life is at work in you" (II Corinthians 4:10-12).

This includes the willingness to come with a "self-destroying prophecy."

Nineveh is lost. Only if Jonah becomes a sacrament can this city be saved.

What does sacramental living look like in your life?

DAY TWELVE

⁓

*"But the LORD provided a great fish to swallow Jonah,
and Jonah was inside the fish three days and three
nights" (Jonah 1:17).*

*T*he only answer God has for Nineveh's problem drowns.
Only if Jonah becomes a sacrament can Nineveh be saved!
This act of Jonah was not voluntary. He was not a martyr. A
martyr is a witness who has a choice—deny Christ and live, or proclaim Christ and be killed. There are many Christians killed each
year because of their ethnicity or religion. There are a few martyrs
who die with a witness for Jesus on their lips.

It has been my privilege to serve the persecuted church for more
than 50 years. I've visited churches in the former Soviet Union, in
China, in Cuba, in Colombia, and in many Muslim countries. And
I have discovered that there is only one way to end persecution of
Christians—stop talking about Jesus.

If we want to see people reached for Jesus, to see the Gospel
transform lives, there is a price that must be paid. The price: we
must give up our rights. We must live sacramentally. We must die to
ourselves so that Christ can live through us.

When we live this way, we lose our fear. Initiative translated into
bold proclamation removes fear. When you hear God and follow

His command, you can be sure God will put you on the right path.

There are compelling reasons to listen to God's word. It enables you to do things you couldn't do otherwise. Take for example Jesus and the man with the paralyzed arm. With His creative word Jesus says, "Stretch out your arm!" Can the man do that? No! Unless the man acts on the Word of God. The man with the paralyzed arm—he stretches his arm out according to Jesus' Word.

Don't believe what the devil tells you. The devil says "You will always be sinful … poor … sick … etc."

The devil said to Jonah in the belly of the fish: "You will never get out of here. You'll die in this smelly, stinking fish."

The devil is a liar. Even when he tells the truth.

Never believe what the devil says.

Another example is in the New Testament.

Lazarus died. Jesus wasn't there…or he would not have died.

Jesus confronts death. And He speaks

A mighty word.

A powerful word.

A creative word.

A life-giving word.

The word was so powerful that if He hadn't said Lazarus's name first, ALL the dead would have risen.

The word of God comes again to Jonah.

But first a word to the fish: spit Jonah out.

The fish won't argue with God.

Jonah could say no. So can you. But how much better it is when we say "yes."

Is God calling to you? What is your answer?

_____

_____

_____

_____

_____

_____

_____

_____

_____

_____

_____

_____

_____

_____

DAY THIRTEEN

"From inside the fish Jonah prayed to the LORD his God. He said: 'In my distress I called to the LORD, and he answered me. From the depths of the grave I called for help, and you listened to my cry'" (Jonah 2:1-2).

Jonah's mission allowed him some unique privileges. He became the first human to ride in a submarine and to sleep on a foam blubber bed.

I don't think Jonah was impressed.

How did he feel in the fish? Desperate, no doubt. We see it in Jonah's prayer.

There are some who believe that Jonah died and was brought back to life. Others make the argument that Jonah could have survived three days in the fish and cite historic examples. Whether or not Jonah actually died is not the issue. The reality is that Jonah thought he had died. When he was thrown into the sea, he believed that was the end of his journey. At least, he probably thought, he wouldn't have to go to Nineveh.

Within the fish, Jonah could do only one thing: pray. And so Jonah's greatest weakness became his greatest strength. He had no more physical strength. He could no longer run from God. He had lost everything. In his distress Jonah prayed. That's not strong enough. "From the depths of the grave" he prayed. Jonah cried for help, and God listened.

Jonah proves you can pray anytime, wherever you are. God hears! And God does not laugh at Jonah's prayer.

He was running from the presence of God. But Jonah discovers that you can't escape from God's presence. "Where can I go from your Spirit?" wrote the psalmist. "Where can I flee from your presence? If I go up to the heavens, you are there; if I make my bed in the depths, you are there" (Psalm 139:7-8). You can't get more in the depths than Jonah, tossed wildly about as the fish swam through the sea.

It doesn't pay to run from God. I hope you aren't running from God. Jesus won't stop you from running away. But it will be very lonely. It will be very dark. It will be very dangerous. And you won't escape from Him.

God pursued Jonah for the sake of Nineveh. But there are other occasions where God let the person run. Consider the sad case of the rich young ruler who came to Jesus. Jesus said, "Sell your possessions and give to the poor... Then come, follow me." The young ruler couldn't do that and walked away from Jesus. Our Lord never took one step after him (Matthew 19:16-24).

So be careful. The pull of money or prestige or a girlfriend or a career may take you away from the call of God. You can run away. Or you can cry out to God. If you will call to the Lord, He is there.

The measure of my misery when I turn from God is in proportion to my knowledge of Him when I did walk with him. (Oswald Chambers, *Seed Thoughts Calendar*, August 11.)

Are you running from God? Why?

_____
_____
_____
_____
_____
_____
_____
_____
_____
_____
_____
_____
_____
_____
_____
_____

DAY FOURTEEN

"You hurled me into the deep, into the very heart of the seas, and the currents swirled about me; all your waves and breakers swept over me. I said, 'I have been banished from your sight; yet I will look again toward your holy temple'" (Jonah 2:3-4).

How did it feel sliding down the beast's throat to a splash landing in the gastric juices of the belly? Then the beast dives into the depths, makes a sudden turn after a school of fish, gobbles down some minnows mixed with seaweed, then tears back up towards the surface. No roller coaster had more twists and turns, but Jonah's ride was a terror, not a thrill. It occurred in utter darkness. No wonder he felt "I have been banished from your sight."

In the belly of the ship, Jonah had slept while the sailors held a prayer meeting. Now in the belly of the fish, Jonah has a unique prayer encounter. He struggles not with the elements, but with the Lord of Nature. "You hurled me into the deep," Jonah says. Not the sailors. God! Here, when all hope is lost, Jonah acknowledges the Lordship of God.

He is Lord of the heavens and Lord of the earth. Lord of the land and the sea. Jonah has to acknowledge that truth. The Lord directed the storm to the exact spot where Jonah's ship was sailing.

And God commanded the fish to pick Jonah up the moment he was tossed into the sea. Jonah doesn't believe he will see land again—he will end his life as fish food. With no other options, Jonah finally recognizes that God is Lord of his life. You cannot acknowledge Him as Lord and not do what He tells you.

That's why we can never say, "No, Lord!" It's a contradiction. Lordship requires obedience. If we shake our fist at God and rebel against His commands, He lets us run. But He is Lord of all nature, and eventually we may be forced to submit. Peter in Acts had a vision of a sheet descending from Heaven with numerous unclean animals. "Kill and eat." he was told. "Surely not, Lord!" said Peter, "I have never eaten anything impure or unclean." (Acts 10:13b-14) He was not going to save the heathen Romans. But God repeated the vision and Peter got the message. Rather than run away, Peter went to Caesarea and brought God's message to the centurion Cornelius and his family. Jesus is Lord and Peter recognized that he must obey.

Jonah struggles to surrender to the Lordship of God. I struggle, too. Are we going to run away? Or are we going to submit?

We pray: Thy kingdom come, thy will be done on earth as it is in heaven.

Are we serious when we pray those words? Are we willing to be part of God's answer to that prayer?

I can't help but notice that it never occurred to Jonah to pray for Nineveh.

Where in your life are you not submitting to God's Lordship?

*"The engulfing waters threatened me, the deep
surrounded me; seaweed was wrapped around my head.
To the roots of the mountains I sank down; the earth
beneath barred me in forever. But you brought my life
up from the pit, O LORD my God" (Jonah 2:5-6).*

*W*hat would Jonah have wanted in this grave? Perhaps a Bible?
Probably a reading light? It was pitch black. He didn't have
a flashlight—it wouldn't have worked anyway. If he'd had a pocket
testament, saltwater would have stuck the pages together, and the
gastric acid of the fish would have eaten away at the edges.

Sliding around in the belly of the fish Jonah had nothing to grab
hold of—except for the Word of God which he'd already memorized
and hidden in his heart.

There is nothing original about Jonah's prayer. It's straight out
of Scripture. Listen to this from Psalm 18, "The cords of death
entangled me; the torrents of destruction overwhelmed me. The
cords of the grave coiled around me; the snares of death confronted
me. In my distress I called to the LORD; I cried to my God for help"
(Psalm 18:4-6). It's not an exact quotation, but you see the pattern.
And there's more. In his prayer Jonah draws from Psalms 31, 50, 69,
and 142.

Do you have the resources of Scripture to draw from if you were to find yourself in desperate circumstances without a Bible? In the March 12, 1973 issue of TIME magazine, there was an article about the prisoners of war being held in "the Hanoi Hilton." The prisoners had as one of their major projects to reconstruct a Bible from their collective memory. Anyone who could recall biblical passages contributed. I've often wondered how thick was that Bible? How thick would mine would be if I were in a similar situation?

Over the years I've met with many Christians who have spent time in prison because of their faith. Those who had the most Scripture memorized seemed to survive the best. Wang Ming Dao spent 23 years in prison. He said, "If I'd known I would spend 23 years without a Bible, I would have spent much more time memorizing Scripture."

When you reach your darkest hours, what will give you strength?

"I have hidden your word in my heart that I might not sin against you" (Psalm 119:11).

If you were in prison without a copy of the scriptures, how thick would your Bible be?

DAY SIXTEEN

"I said, 'I have been banished from your sight;
yet I will look again toward your holy temple'"
(Jonah 2:4).

"When my life was ebbing away, I remembered you,
LORD, and my prayer rose to you, to your holy temple"
(Jonah 2:7).

Twice Jonah refers to the temple. I wonder if Jonah had ever seen it. Given that he lived in northern Israel, and that the temple resided to the South in Jerusalem, and that Israel and Judah were enemies, it's possible that Jonah had never been to the temple. However, tradition insisted that when he prayed he face Jerusalem. That probably began with Solomon when during the dedication of the temple he prayed, "Hear the supplication of your servant and of your people Israel when they pray toward this place" (I Kings 8:30a). Daniel prayed three times daily on his knees at his window that faced toward Jerusalem.

Why was this so important? Because God was in the temple. So Jonah believed. When the kingdom of David was divided, people in the Northern kingdom could no longer make the annual trip to the temple. The best they could do was pray in that direction.

When Jesus met the Samaritan woman at the well in Sychar,

she said, "Our fathers worshiped on this mountain, but you Jews claim that the place where we must worship is in Jerusalem." Jesus responded that a time was coming when true worshipers would worship the Father in spirit and truth.

In the belly of the fish—Jonah couldn't get on his knees, nor could he pray in the right direction. Still, God heard his prayer.

And God hears our prayers today, not because of the position of our body or the direction we face—Muslims believe God only hears their prayers if they are facing Mecca. "Don't you know that you yourselves are God's temple and that God's Spirit lives in you? If anyone destroys God's temple, God will destroy him; for God's temple is sacred, and you are that temple" (I Corinthians 3:16-17).

Jonah's focus was on the temple in Jerusalem. He didn't see the Ninevites as potential temples.

Do we see members of al Qaeda or Hamas as potential temples of the Holy Spirit?

They won't be if we don't pray for them, and if someone in whom Christ dwells doesn't go to them.

It's no easier for us than it was for Jonah.

Who among the lost needs your prayers? Take some time to pray for them now.

DAY SEVENTEEN

⁓

"Those who cling to worthless idols forfeit the grace that could be theirs. But I, with a song of thanksgiving, will sacrifice to you. What I have vowed I will make good" (*Jonah 2:8-9a*).

*W*hat makes Jonah think that he will escape from the belly of the great fish?

In the midst of his desperate prayer, Jonah finds hope: "You brought my life up from the pit, O LORD my God." Jonah has no hope of rescue by worthless idols. His only hope is that God, the Ruler of Nature, rescues him. And if He does, Jonah promises a song of thanksgiving. And what he has vowed he will make good. What has he vowed? We can imagine that he probably vowed to obey God. "Okay, Lord, if you rescue me I'll go to Nineveh." There, that was settled! It wasn't said with much enthusiasm. It was a statement of resignation rather than joy. However anything was better than being stuck in the belly of this fish. Even Nineveh?

Jonah certainly didn't feel thankful in his circumstances. He was still sloshing around in the mix of seawater, seaweed and plankton. But he'd turned a corner.

We can learn what Jonah learned. Do not be guided by your fear. Do not be guided by your frustration. Do not be guided by your preconceived ideas. Proclaim the value of quoting God's

Word—even in the whale/jail house. The Holy Spirit then becomes responsible to bring that Word to pass.

Jonah needed to die to learn this lesson. We learn this lesson by dying on the cross. "I have been crucified with Christ" (Galatians 2:20). This is what Muslims need to learn. A crucified man can never risk his life anymore, because he has lost all fear. So now we are free to go wherever God tells us to go. Even to Iraq.

We should not wear the cross as a necklace but as our life. A cross on a chain is only a piece of jewelry. What does it show the world? The cross is meant to offend—not by adorning a musician singing a profane song, but rather in the surrender of a life to the Lordship of Jesus, who died for us and rose again.

There is only one way God saves—through the cross.

That is what we must preach, but that preaching is only effective if we've died on that cross first.

What are the areas of your life that you need to die to?

DAY EIGHTEEN

⁓

Salvation comes from the LORD" (Jonah 2:9b).

This is what we proclaim: Salvation is of the Lord!

Proclamation always offers the solution to a problem. We have the answer to the problem of sin. The wickedness of Nineveh came before the Lord. Today the sins of the world still come before God. Not generalities. Specific sins like stealing, murder, adultery, pride, and in affluence not taking care of the poor. We all have sinned. I have sinned. I'm not going to tell you my sins. Only that salvation is for my *specific* sins. And for yours as well.

Why is the world rising up in protest against injustice? We demand answers to the problem of terrorism. To the problem of violence in schools. To the problem of economic exploitation of brick workers in Pakistan. To the sexual exploitation of women and children in too many parts of the world. We must preach the solution. We will not solve problems of violence with violence. We will not solve the problem of terrorism by simply killing terrorists. "The fruit of righteousness will be peace; the effect of righteousness will be quietness and confidence forever" (Isaiah 32:17). But for righteousness to take effect there must first be repentance and a massive turning to God. That is why Jonah preached. That is why we must preach.

Jonah was going to a violent city. God sent Jonah to Nineveh to demonstrate what He wants to do with the whole world. First, there is judgment for our sins. Nineveh will be destroyed. Unless...

There is also forgiveness, if we repent. The demands of justice are fulfilled on the cross. This is what we must preach!

But you ask how are you, how am I, qualified to preach?

Look at the Apostle Paul. He was least of the apostles (I Corinthians 15:9). He was least of all the saints (Ephesians 3:8). And he was greatest of all sinners (I Timothy 1:15). But he met the perfect Savior.

Isn't that our story? Aren't we all called to do this? Preaching is the function of the Church, which exists for the salvation of its non-members.

"If in your preaching you do not deal with the contemporary problems, then you are not preaching the good news at all" (Martin Luther).

The Bible is full of questions, all to be answered in Jesus!

Who in your life needs to hear the message of repentance and forgiveness?

_____

_____

_____

_____

_____

_____

_____

_____

_____

_____

_____

_____

_____

DAY NINETEEN

⁓

"And the LORD commanded the fish, and it vomited Jonah onto dry land" (Jonah 2:10).

"Then the word of the LORD came to Jonah a second time" (Jonah 3:1).

*H*ave you ever prayed for a second chance? You come to a place of hopelessness because you didn't pray and now you wonder: will God give me a second chance if I pray?

At the end of his prayer the fish could no longer stomach Jonah. The fish vomited Jonah onto the beach. How the prophet appreciated the sand—he never thought he'd feel solid ground beneath him again. He barely opened his eyes, then shut them again—the sun was so bright that his eyes had to adjust. Slowly he caught his breath. He turned over onto his back and finally opened his eyes. What a beautiful sight—the Mediterranean Sea spread out before him. Not a cloud in the sky. No hint of a storm. He turned around and looked up at the trees lining the hills. That was even more beautiful—in fact, he wouldn't mind if he never again set foot on a boat.

To one side was a stream and Jonah went over to wash off the sand and residue of vomit, dead fish and seaweed. As he washed himself in the fresh water, he happened to notice his reflection in a still pool. Who was that horrible creature? He looked up and saw a child staring at him on the beach. The child started to cry, then turned and ran away.

Jonah finished his bath, but the smell was still horrible. His clothes. What was left of them—they needed to be washed. He stripped and plunged his coat into the water, then scrubbed it on a rock, and finally set it on a bush to dry.

Then he heard a voice. "Jonah!" It was his Boss.

The word of the Lord came to Jonah a second time. Go to Nineveh. Jonah wasn't going to disobey God again. He had a good twenty-day walk ahead of him. He'd better get started. The coat wasn't dry yet, but he quickly threw it over his body and started walking east.

Jonah was in the belly of a fish because of disobedience, rebellion, and faithlessness. Jonah thought in terms of "I" and not of God. But God forgave and re-commissioned Jonah. Jonah did not deserve his second chance!

I'll tell you a secret: Jonah did not deserve his first chance either. None of us deserve to be in God's kingdom. None of us are worthy servants.

It's all by grace!

God does not reprimand me for my failure, my unbelief, my disobedience, or my delayed obedience. All the wrongs I have done have already turned into self-inflicted punishments: I know I brought this great suffering on myself.

God, please forgive me.

You still love me.

You will start again with me.

Go and preach. Those are also the words Jesus gave His disciples. And those are our instructions today.

You cannot spell Gospel or God without first spelling Go.

Is there somewhere God is calling you to go? Where?
When will you go?

DAY TWENTY

"Go to the great city of Nineveh and proclaim to it the message I give you" (Jonah 3:2).

Jonah goes to Nineveh not to entertain but to proclaim. And his preaching is the solution to the terrorism of the Assyrians. Think about it. The northern kingdom of Israel had struggled to solve the problem of the Assyrians. They had debated various solutions. Should they attempt to work through diplomatic channels—registering protests in all of the courts of all the neighboring counties? Or should they launch an economic boycott—it would certainly hurt the Assyrians if the trade routes through Israel and Judah were blocked. Or should they attempt to destroy them militarily? King Jeroboam II had seen some military success, but could his forces stand against the most powerful military in the world? And would his people support him if the campaign lasted several years? How many Israelite children would die before the people protested and demanded that their sons come home?

None of these options seemed attractive. Jonah knew. He'd heard all of them argued by the king's advisors. Now Jonah was going to Nineveh, but he was not carrying diplomatic papers from the king. Jonah's orders came from a higher authority. Go and preach!

When did preaching ever solve the problem of terrorism? Jonah had heard the hawks say over and over, "the only thing those Assyrians understand is force."

God had told Jonah to go to Nineveh and preach against it. Jonah ran away, and look at all the problems that his anger caused him. So now Jonah obeyed, and this time the instructions were more specific. "Go and proclaim the message I give you," God said.

God was taking no chances. Well, if anything, that made Jonah's job easier. He didn't have to find a singing group to draw a crowd. He didn't have to defend Israel's political position. He wasn't going to worry about having a program for the youth so the adults could listen uninterrupted. He didn't even consider writing a couple of jokes to warm up the audience. This would be a no-frills campaign. God wanted him to preach one message. He would do that and no more.

God was taking greater share of the responsibility by not only limiting the message, but by telling Jonah exactly what the message was.

I wonder, are we allowed to preach anything other than what Jesus tells us?

In a time of crisis we must not entertain. We must warn!

The word we give is His word.

The place where we go is His choice.

Whatever results we see are His results.

Whose message are you preaching? God's or your own?
What is that message?

_____

_____

_____

_____

_____

_____

_____

_____

_____

_____

_____

_____

_____

DAY TWENTY-ONE

⌒

"Jonah obeyed the word of the LORD and went to Nineveh" (Jonah 3:3a).

Jonah probably walked to Nineveh. That's approximately 400 miles from the Mediterranean Sea to Assyria's capital city just east of the Tigris River. No one offered him a ride—one look at him and travelers quickly moved away. If he walked twenty miles a day, that's twenty long days.

How did Jonah use the time? He could have planned out some messages, but since God had told him what to say, there were no messages to plan. So he probably did a lot of thinking. Jonah was grateful to be alive. But he was going where he didn't want to go. Going to Assyria. To his enemies. He couldn't help but think of what they had done to his people. And worse, he was traveling there without the permission of King Jeroboam. This would be considered treason, unless...

His message was clear: "In 40 days Nineveh will be destroyed!" This improved Jonah's outlook. How would God do it? It needed to be something horrific—to pay the Assyrians back for all of their terrible atrocities. Probably not a flood—he'd seen a rainbow recently and was reminded that God would not destroy the world again via water. Then probably fire—like Sodom and Gomorrah. Better, how about an earthquake first? Then a giant hail storm. Followed by fire from Heaven to burn up all that remained. No one would be left alive, not even a dog or a cat!

When that happened Jonah could return home a hero. What honors would he receive in the royal court if he could report that Israel's biggest problem was solved? He would love to deliver that message: "Good news, your highness—you don't need to worry about Nineveh anymore!"

But something checked Jonah's spirit. It might not work out so neatly. There was another possibility. The Ninevites might actually listen to Jonah's preaching. And repent. And then... Jonah knew how God worked. This was just like Him. How would he explain that to King Jeroboam? "Your highness, I preached to the Ninevites and they repented and said they would bother us no more." Right! The royal court would mock him and accuse him of treason. Aiding and abetting the enemy. That would probably mean a death sentence.

He would have to convince the king and his royal advisors that this was God's doing, not his. God was responsible. God had rescued him from the storm and from the belly of the fish. Wait a minute: that meant God could protect him from the wrath of the king. Suddenly, he didn't feel any fear. Nothing the king did to him could be worse than what he'd already experienced inside that fish.

Jesus said, "It is not the healthy who need a doctor, but the sick. But go and learn what this means: 'I desire mercy, not sacrifice.' For I have not come to call the righteous, but sinners."(Matthew 9:12-13) How are you taking the Message to the sick? Are you worried about what other Christians will think or say if you are seen preaching to the "enemy"?

DAY TWENTY-TWO

"Now Nineveh was a very important city—a visit required three days" (Jonah 3:3b).

The sun was going down. People were heading home. Many people pressed toward the gate: at dark the gates were closed and the surrounding area was not exactly the safest place on earth. Better be inside the walls; that was bad enough.

Among the tired workers arriving from their fields walked a man, more tired than them all. He looked worn and haggard and his dirty clothing had a peculiar smell to it. You would not want to sit next to him in a crowded restaurant. Or in church! In fact he smelled like a fish market.

He looked even worse. He'd probably lost his eyebrows and beard and much of his hair. His skin was waxy white, as though someone had poured acid over him. Come to think of it, hadn't he recently spent three days bathing in the stomach acid of a fish? So at the end of the day Jonah snuck into the great city, trying to avoid any attention. This was no time to start preaching.

Jonah had a message: 40 days and Nineveh will be destroyed. Could he in good faith count this day as the first day of his mission? Then tomorrow would be day two of Operation Nineveh, and when he started preaching—but where? How? He didn't know. Anyway, when he did start preaching, because he had no choice, maybe, just maybe, he could begin by announcing: "39 more days…!"

He found an inn. He had a long, restless night. His thoughts churned inside him while his body turned over and over again until he longed for daybreak. But that wouldn't bring him relief. He was dreading this day.

Okay he'd give God the benefit of the doubt and call this Day One of Operation Nineveh. He would announce, "40 more days and Nineveh will be destroyed."

Why was Jonah full of fear? What was bothering him? Was it the condition of this city? Clearly they had no knowledge of God. Nineveh was lost—every man, woman, boy and girl was LOST forever.

Today we don't believe that anymore, do we? If we really did, wouldn't we be willing to crawl on our bare knees over a field strewn with broken glass to reach that one lost soul?

Everything we do is based on what we believe. That's true in every criminal act, every act of immorality, every terrorist act—yes, a suicide bomber has a strong sense of belief.

Doing nothing also reveals your opinion. When we take no initiative, when we are not aggressive and the world is overtaken by evil because of what they believe, then evil wins over good.

Jonah knew Nineveh was lost—or did he? He was certainly the only one who could *do* something about it.

So can you. But fear…

The best definition of fear is: False Evidence Appearing Real. Today, we have created an enemy image of Muslims. We fear fundamentalists. We fear the consequences when a Muslim state acquires nuclear weapons. We worry about Muslims immigrating to the West, taking over our neighborhoods, imposing Sharia Law. Isn't that why we fear them?

Or maybe the real reason we fear Muslims is that we won't tell them, "God loves you."

What is it you are afraid of? What fears hold you back from following the Lord? From sharing His love with the lost?

_____

_____

_____

_____

_____

_____

_____

_____

_____

_____

_____

_____

_____

_____

DAY TWENTY-THREE

On the first day, Jonah started into the city. He proclaimed: "Forty more days and Nineveh will be overturned." (Jonah 3:4)

*Q*uestion: If God sent you to Amsterdam to preach, and you had no contact and you didn't know the city, where would you start, and what would you say?

Day One of Operation Nineveh.

Jonah decided he'd start preaching at the souk. That was the marketplace where surrounding farmers came to sell their lettuce, onions and garlic, their eggs, sheep and cattle, their wool, leather and cloth. The souk had two distinct advantages. First, most people were gathered there anyway, the natives and the visitors, so that in one public appearance many would see him. Well, at least from the outside—what his inside, his heart, was like…hopefully they would never find out.

Second, it was terribly busy here. There were so many voices of merchants shouting, trying to sell their goods by out-shouting their competitors, not to mention those noisy animals. So although there was a maximum of exposure, not many would listen anyway.

There was a third advantage to the souk. They sold spices. He established his "pulpit" near that part of the market so that the scents of cinnamon, dill and saffron, along with frankincense, myrrh and nard, would cover up his smell.

So Jonah fulfilled his part of the deal: day one was accomplished. Thirty-nine more to go.

As he walked away from the market, he saw a little girl standing in a doorway, clutching a ragged wool doll, staring at him. And behind the girl, a woman. Also staring at him. With tears streaming down her face.

Day Seven of Operation Nineveh.

The Sabbath. Glory Hallelujah! Jonah never felt happier with the fourth commandment than on this day. He had no intention of breaking God's holy law. Of the law of love he'd never yet heard. How could he...

Or had he? What was that again in Exodus 34:6? "The LORD... abounding in love." Away with it! No one can tamper with the Ten Commandments when they are so clear. If today his calf or goat or even his favorite dog would fall into the well, Jonah would not—and I repeat: he would *not* pull the poor creature out of the water. On the Sabbath you don't work. Period!

The people, some of them at least, missed him. He had become kind of familiar to them; that odd man with the bleached skin, no hair and a frightening message.

What did they know about the Jewish religion anyway, much less about the Sabbath? Well, everyone seemed to have a "back to normal" day, almost. There was just a tiny, little nagging doubt in Jonah's heart: today people here would die, and no one would tell them...

Never had a day off seemed so long and restless to the prophet of God. Even some people in the city thought it was a long day. The little girl with the doll stopped crying. And her mother thought all day about the odd man's message.

Where shall you take God's message? Where do you begin?

DAY TWENTY-FOUR

"The Ninevites believed God. They declared a fast, and all of them, from the greatest to the least, put on sackcloth" (Jonah 3:5)

Word about the strange prophet spread. People who heard him at the souk went home and told their families and neighbors.

Meanwhile Jonah advanced through the huge city. Anywhere he found a noisy crowd, he stopped to deliver his message.

"Thirty more days and Nineveh will be destroyed."

"Twenty more days and Nineveh will be destroyed."

"Ten more days…"

Jonah had no program. All he did was preach the Word God gave him. And an amazing thing happened. People stopped to listen to the stranger. Then they started talking. "Suppose what he says is true?" said one. "I think he really means it," said another. "Maybe we'd better do something." "Maybe *I'd* better do something."

They took action. Perhaps that woman and her daughter with the rag doll were the first to grab some burlap bags from the souk. Her husband and neighbors quickly followed their example. Right there by the souk where Jonah preached his first message they put on their sackcloth and sat in front of their homes.

"What are you doing?" one of the merchants asked.

"Didn't you listen to the prophet?" the woman said.

"You mean that crazy man with the bleached skin condition?"

"That man isn't crazy. He said our city would be destroyed. I tell you, God is judging us and we deserve it. We need to pray urgently. I'm dressing in burlap to demonstrate we are truly sorry for our wickedness."

Soon many others were making the sackcloth fashion statement. This was real repentance. They were confessing their sins and calling on God to forgive them. It was a miracle!

Do we really believe God can work that way today? Why not?

We live in a very troubled world. War. Hunger. Persecution. Racism. Crime. Islamic fundamentalism. Suicide bombers.

The Bible says that the real underlying problem is SIN. And God did something about it. The prophets proclaimed that a dire situation can change IF people will believe them. If we repent, if we believe God's message, we could see the miracle of Nineveh repeated today.

The Apostle Paul wrote: "God was pleased through the foolishness of what was preached to save those who believe" (I Corinthians 1:21b).

Something happens when people hear the Word of God. The totally lost can be totally saved because of the perfect Savior.

We who preach the Gospel are the most effective instruments to fight terrorism in the world. Because forgiven people are changed people, and they don't blow other people up.

Do you believe God can still drastically change lives today? Do you really want him to? Why or why not?

_____

_____

_____

_____

_____

_____

_____

_____

_____

_____

_____

_____

DAY TWENTY-FIVE

"When the news reached the king of Nineveh, he rose from his throne, took off his royal robes, covered himself with sackcloth and sat down in the dust" (Jonah 3:6).

*Q*uestion: Can a city really change that fast?

Answer: It can change as fast as a person can change.

The people who heard Jonah preach told everyone they knew. Some of them worked in the palace. They told the servants who talked with the guards. One of the guards told his captain who reported this to the head of security. The head of security told it to one of the king's advisors who passed it along to the entire cabinet. The king saw his advisors discussing the situation and wanted to know what they were talking about.

God gave us a message: His Word. It is so strong that a person is transformed from being an alcoholic, or a drug addict, or a criminal. Or a terrorist.

The drug addict: free!

The alcoholic: delivered!

The criminal: converted!

If we effectively reach people on the street, like Jonah did, the fundamentalists of Taliban or Al Qaeda or Hamas or Islamic Jihad can become peaceful followers of Jesus.

Then peace can come to the city, the land, the world.

A few years ago I was on a radio talk show with a Jewish host who challenged me with this question: "Suppose, when you die, you discover that what you preach is not true?"

I answered, "Michael, after all you've done, when you die suppose you discover that the Gospel *is* true. I'm afraid all of the risk is on you!"

Nineveh believed that Jonah just might be right. Better be safe and repent!

We need to get God's message out today. Everyone needs to hear it. People often comment on how brave I am to go and meet with leaders of terrorist groups and tell them about Jesus. I disagree. That doesn't require courage; only obedience. There is nothing I have done that you could not have done, or said, or believed. I have often said, "If I, a simple Dutchman, can go and do this, then a million people can do it."

Becoming a Christian means entering into freedom.

But freedom for one thing only: freedom to obey our Master.

Are you in living in freedom? What is the evidence?

*"Then he issued a proclamation in Nineveh:
'By the decree of the king and his nobles:
Do not let any man or beast, herd or flock, taste
anything; do not let them eat or drink. But let man
and beast be covered with sackcloth. Let everyone call
urgently on God. Let them give up their evil ways and
their violence. Who knows? God may yet relent and
with compassion turn from his fierce anger so that we
will not perish'" (Jonah 3:7-9).*

The people of Nineveh have a prayer meeting. They repent. They fast. The animals become very quiet—their throats are so dry. Every person and beast is covered with sackcloth. And the people wonder: "Who knows?"

You and I have questions. God knows the answers.

We all believe we live in the end times. But we don't know for sure.

We know death is a certainty, but we don't know when.

Who knows what God will do in you? Who knows what God will do in the Muslim world?

Nineveh cries out for mercy, for forgiveness. This is the reaction God looks for everywhere.

We see it in other parts of Scripture. The prophet Joel announced:

"Blow the trumpet in Zion; sound the alarm, on my holy hill. Let all who live in the land tremble, for the day of the LORD is coming… 'Even now,' declares the LORD, "return to me with all your heart, with fasting and weeping and mourning.' Rend your heart and not your garments. Return to the LORD your God, for he is gracious and compassionate, slow to anger and abounding in love, and he relents from sending calamity" (Joel 2:1, 12-13)

Joel concludes: "Who knows? He may turn and have pity and leave behind a blessing."

God says He will destroy Nineveh. But *who knows*? Maybe if they repent, change their ways…. Jonah wasn't that good of a preacher, yet the people repented. And God changed his mind.

Here's one thing we do know; much of the world is now where Nineveh would have been without Jonah: LOST. And of that world, there are some 1.5 billion people, the Islamic world, that may be preparing for a massive assault on us! They call it Jihad.

Does it have to be? No! God can use you. He can use me. What will happen when God uses ordinary people? What will happen if we love Muslims and tell them about Jesus? Who knows?

"Despise not man or things
however weak or small
God loves to use and mightily use
What man counts nothing at all."
    (C.T. Studd, missionary)

Is God's arm shortened that it cannot save? (Isaiah 59:1)

As an ordinary person, how are you allowing God to use you?

DAY TWENTY-SEVEN

"When God saw what they did and how they turned from their evil ways, he had compassion and did not bring upon them the destruction he had threatened" (Jonah 3:10).

*O*peration Nineveh, Day 40.

Even the leaves on the trees do not move. There is no wind. A deathly quiet has settled over the city. The cows are not lowing—thirst has killed their instinct to complain about the extreme harshness of life.

Traffic has come to a complete standstill. The shops are closed. Nothing moves. You can cut the heavy silence; it almost has a body. In front of the houses many families have gathered, father and mother, desperate expressions on their faces, yet not altogether without hope. But where would help come from? Mother carries a baby, the other children hold on to her skirt. Father has his hands spread out, palms forward, as if in a gesture of surrender, but to whom?

The only one moving is the stranger, who is no longer a stranger. Actually, he remains a stranger because the people of Nineveh never really got to know him. But then who wanted to know a man who did not show any love for them? He never answered their questions.

Jonah is moving toward the east gate. There a road leads up the hill. He arrived 40 days ago at the west gate. Now his mission is finished. Operation Nineveh is…

A failure!

God saw what the people of Nineveh did. He saw their sincere repentance. And so God changed His mind. God did not destroy Nineveh.

That was Jonah's problem. In the Middle East nothing is worse than losing face—to be shamed. God made him look like a fool. Jonah's prophecy did not come true. After forty days Nineveh remained standing. The people weren't cursing but singing. They visibly changed and so God changed His mind.

Surely this is one of the greatest miracles of history. Wouldn't you be excited if you preached one sermon and an entire city repented and crime was eliminated and the terrorist threat to your nation no longer existed?

But who is preaching that sermon?

Maybe we need to pray. Is there a harvest of souls in the Muslim world? If so, we should "Ask the Lord of the harvest, therefore, to send out workers into his harvest field" (Matthew 9:38).

Where are the places in your life in which you are too concerned
about losing face and not willing to speak God's message?

_____

_____

_____

_____

_____

_____

_____

_____

_____

_____

_____

_____

_____

_____

DAY TWENTY-EIGHT

"But Jonah was greatly displeased and became angry"
(Jonah 4:1).

There is a story about a teacher who asked her Sunday school class, "Who wants to go to Heaven?" Little Johnny immediately raised his hand. When the teacher recognized him, he answered: "I want to go to Heaven, but not with this bunch."

I think that was Jonah's sentiment. It is day forty-one. The day after Nineveh should have disappeared from the face of the earth. Apparently God has saved these people that Jonah hated. Did that mean he was going to have to spend eternity with this bunch of heathens?

God is interested in the "day before the day after." Because of what happened the day before, God did not fulfill His threat. Jonah shouldn't have been surprised. He knew what the people of Nineveh did not, that the Lord Almighty had revealed Himself to Moses as "the compassionate and gracious God, slow to anger, abounding in love and faithfulness, maintaining love to thousands, and forgiving wickedness, rebellion and sin. Yet he does not leave the guilty unpunished" (Exodus 34:6-7a).

If you'd only memorize and remember *this* verse it would be your guiding light in life, helping you to love God and accept His forgiveness. Then you'd believe that God can change and save not only your loved ones but also your adversaries!

That was Jonah's problem. He refused to believe that God could save Muslims and transform Muslim fundamentalists into peace-loving pacifists.

Yes, Jonah was very angry, and he said so. His anger was based on what he knew about God. Yes, he knew God is gracious, merciful, slow to anger. But that doesn't mean God can't also be angry. God's anger is specifically mentioned 177 times in the Bible! By contrast human anger is only mentioned 45 times. But then God has a lot more reason to be angry than we do.

Jonah is angry because God's love is manifested in a heathen enemy city. "But look at my own country!" Jonah could protest. "Why do I see miracles in a heathen land and not at home? How can you save Nineveh while Israel goes to hell? Is it right that I preach to a non-covenant people and you save them, whereas I preach in Israel and they do not get saved?"

Here at home we also have unbelief, manifesting itself in broken homes, separated families, collapsed morals, violence and crime on the streets. One mother's son is on drugs. Another man's wife is an alcoholic. A Christian businessman goes broke because his partner stole company funds. Government officials are corrupt. Television broadcasts a steady stream of immoral content. And You save Nineveh God? Why? That's not fair! How can You do that?

God's answer: The people of Nineveh *did* something! They met My conditions. They repented, *all* of them. They turned from their evil ways. And they didn't wait until the last day to do it.

I once heard a story about a boy who asked his rabbi, "When shall I repent?" The rabbi replied, "One day before your death." The boy protested, "But I don't know that day." The rabbi responded, "that's why you must do it *today*!"

Don't wait. Do it Today!

*What is it you need to say or do **today**?*

DAY TWENTY-NINE

*"He prayed to the L*ORD*, 'O L*ORD*, is this not what
I said when I was still at home? That is why I was so
quick to flee to Tarshish. I knew that you are a gracious
and compassionate God, slow to anger and abounding
in love, a God who relents from sending calamity'"*
(Jonah 4:2).

Jonah preached judgment to Nineveh. We love to condemn our enemies. Isn't that why there is so much war? We are determined to fight God's wars and we're always so sure that God is on our side.

We should not be so confident that we *are* on God's side. If we were, if we truly agreed with God, we would be witnesses to all the world for Jesus Christ.

Jonah suspected all along what God would do with Nineveh. He knew in Jonah 1:1 when the Word of the Lord came to him. That's why he ran away from God. Jonah knew that if he preached the Word of God, Nineveh would repent. Then God would be gracious and He would forgive.

He will do the same for you—if you repent and turn from sin.

How did Jonah know? It was in his Bible. Jonah's prayer sounds amazingly similar to the revelation of God to Moses in Exodus 34:6-7. Jonah knew about God because he knew God's Book.

If we know God and love God, then we will…
> know His Book,
> love His Book,
> obey His Book.

Jonah knew the Book, but he still argued with God. Obedience is not automatic. We need to strive to understand God and His Book. The amazing thing is that God is so patient with Jonah. He even answers Jonah.

Jonah can argue with God and God doesn't condemn him.

"Know His Book, love His Book, obey His Book," which of these do you need to work on? How will you begin?

_____

_____

_____

_____

_____

_____

_____

_____

_____

_____

_____

_____

_____

DAY THIRTY

*"'Now, O L*ORD*, take away my life, for it is
better for me to die than to live.'
But the L*ORD *replied, 'Have you any right
to be angry?'" (Jonah 4:3-4).*

God has a solution for every problem. Jonah has a problem for
every solution.

For example, Jonah hates the Assyrians, even after they repent.
He refuses to give up his hate. God, however, loves Nineveh. He will
not let a person, a nation, the world go to hell without a warning.
Jonah's problem: He doesn't want to provide the warning.

To save the world, God sent His Son to die. Jonah: he'd rather
die than see Nineveh saved.

Jonah has a problem with God's plan for salvation. Jonah's plan
includes only the Jews. God's plan includes Jews *and* their enemies.
"Is God the God of the Jews only? Is he not also the God of Gentiles too? Yes, of Gentiles too" (Romans 3:29). So God's claim on
Nineveh is as strong as His claim on Jerusalem.

But just how do we get rid of hatred? Jesus said to love your
enemies. Because if you love them, they are no longer your enemies!

Jonah doesn't want to preach to his enemies. When he's forced to do so, he still refuses to love them. In essence he tells God, "You can't make me love them!"

God forgives Nineveh. Jonah doesn't want them forgiven; he wants them judged.

God has a question for Jonah: "Have you any right to be angry?" Jonah doesn't answer God. He walks away.

God is saying, "I have only one plan for the world. That plan includes Nineveh. I only have one message: a message of love and of judgment on those who refuse to believe." God says, "I am sending people out into the world to invite all the nations: including Syria, Iraq, Iran, Afghanistan, Saudi Arabia…

"Jonah if you won't go to Nineveh because they are your enemies, then I have no reserves. You're my plan A and my plan B."

This is so important that Jesus made it his final command: Go into all the world.

God's thinking is so much bigger than ours. We still have not realized how great this salvation is, for us, and for the world. We ought to shout it from every roof top!

In my Dutch language translation of the Bible, Jesus tells the disciples that He *had* to suffer, He *had* to rise from the dead on the third day, and repentance and remission of sin *had* to be preached in His name to all nations, beginning at Jerusalem. (Luke 24:46-47)

Leave out any nation and you upset the balance, and people will turn to other religions and other gods. Even God cannot save anyone outside of Jesus.

Why do we have so little faith? Because we do not obey the clear commands of God. God says He wants to answer our prayers for people to be saved, and that miracles would follow our faith. But we complain that God doesn't answer prayer. However, we haven't obeyed. Jonah didn't even pray for the salvation of Nineveh. Imagine the joy if he had—God was prepared to answer that prayer! He answered it anyway.

So Jonah, do you have any right to be angry? You have only the right to obey. Leave the rest to Me.

Jonah didn't answer God's question.

Disobedience has no answer. Except to run away.

Do you feel your faith is lacking because you don't see God answering your prayers? Is it possible you haven't prayed according to what is on God's heart? How will you find out what is on God's heart? Start today and pray accordingly.

DAY THIRTY-ONE

⌒

"Jonah went out and sat down at a place east of the city"
(Jonah 4:5a).

Jonah sits east of the city, just in case. Why east? He wants to see the sun set on Nineveh. He wants God to keep His promise—alright, fulfill His threat—and destroy the city. Then Jonah's thirst for revenge would be fulfilled. And the threat of the Assyrians to his beloved homeland would be removed. Literally!

After all Jonah had been through, after 40 days of preaching, after the greatest revival in history with the entire city repenting in sackcloth and ashes, shouldn't Jonah have gone out the west gate? Why west? So he could see the sun rise on a new Nineveh. A Nineveh that was no longer wicked. A Nineveh that was no longer a threat to his beloved homeland. Imagine going home and telling his king that the problem of the Assyrians was solved? That's right, the terrorist threat was gone.

But Jonah didn't really want a solution. He wanted revenge. He wanted total annihilation. He wanted proof that Nineveh would no longer threaten his people, and what better proof could there be than a black hole where the great city had once been?

I wonder; are we any more interested in real solutions to today's conflicts?

God's solution: Changed lives. The world's answer: bullets and bombs. Which one is more powerful?

President Lincoln was once asked why he spoke some kind words about his enemies when he should destroy them. Lincoln responded: "I destroy my enemies when I make them my friends."

Who are the enemies in your life who need to become your friends?

DAY THIRTY-TWO

*"There he made himself a shelter, sat in its shade
and waited to see what would happen to the city"
(Jonah 4:5b).*

Jonah is going to wait a long time. God isn't going to change His mind. Because He *already* changed His mind. He will not execute judgment on Nineveh because Nineveh met His conditions for salvation and protection.

When any person or group meets God's conditions, they are automatically entitled to God's protection.

Repentance means we go back to God's rules. We simply need to fit into God's plan to become participants in His power. "Righteousness exalts a nation" not just an individual.

How long is Jonah prepared to wait? He's still going to be waiting when he's ready for a retirement home. Jonah is waiting—for a negative. God is acting—on a positive.

God's love for Nineveh is evidence of His desire and ability to save *every* hostile city and nation.

God can save Baghdad and Kabul. He can save Amsterdam and London. He can save Detroit and Las Vegas.

Jonah is very far from the example of Jesus. "You have prepared a body for me," Jesus said. "Behold I have come to do your will, O God" (Hebrews 10:5b, 7b).

Following the example of Jesus: God has prepared a body. Jonah's body. My body. Your body. Look in the mirror. God has prepared *you*! To do what? To seek and to save the LOST. The parable of the lost sheep shows us: there are 99 reasons for going after that one stray sheep. What an encouragement. That means the shepherd will go after *me* if I go astray.

Likewise the story of Nineveh should encourage us. If God can save Nineveh, He can save any city.

If God has done something on which the salvation of the whole world depends, and if I know it, then I have no choice. I must proclaim it, live for it, suffer for it. And be willing to die for it.

In Heaven, I'd rather be told off for loving too much than for loving too little.

Do you live in (or near) a city God wants to save? What are you doing to help save it?

DAY THIRTY-THREE

*Then the LORD·God provided a vine and made it grow
up over Jonah to give shade for his head to ease his
discomfort, and Jonah was very happy about the vine.
(Jonah 4:6)*

*N*ote the mood swings in this chapter. Jonah was greatly
displeased (v. 1). He was depressed ("LORD, take away my
life" v. 3). Now he is very happy. But give him a couple of more verses
and he will be angry enough to die. I'd say Jonah is rather unstable.

What makes matters worse is that Jonah is angry when he
should be happy. He's witnessed the greatest revival in history and
can't rejoice. But God provides him with a vine and he is ecstatic.
Something is terribly wrong. Jonah is angry that hundreds of thousands are saved. And happy when he has a little air conditioning.

Well, God's vine was certainly more effective than the pitiful
shelter he built. God's vine had big wide leaves that blocked the sun.
His nearly bald head was cool in this shade.

But Jonah's perspective is all wrong. Paul told his protégé that a
good soldier "wants to please his commanding officer" (II Timothy
2:4). That means: stop choosing what pleases us. Love people, use
things. Jonah is still not pleasing the One who has chosen him. But
he loves what God provides for his comfort.

My dear friend Corrie Ten Boom (Author of *The Hiding Place*) helped me learn this valuable lesson. The first time I visited her new home—for years she had traveled the world, living out of a suitcase, and had never had time to settle into her own home in Holland—as I was leaving after a long talk she said to me, "Andrew, keep looking down."

Now I thought that was an odd statement. But Corrie was getting along in years, so I corrected her, saying, "You mean, keep looking up!"

She gave me a fierce look and rebuked me: "No, I mean keep looking down! Look at the world from God's point of view."

I learned more about that perspective on another occasion when my wife and I attended a special concert at the cultural center in Harderwijk. It was a benefit concert for the severely handicapped. We were special guests because one of my sons worked with these handicapped, who were seated in the front row, confined to wheelchairs by physical and mental disabilities. The performance that afternoon was inspiring and I noticed how many of the people in front of me, though unable to speak or clap, moved their bodies in an attempt to feel the music. Between one of the pieces, my wife whispered to me, "Do you think God looks at them and thinks what they could have been?"

That is a very sad thought. Looking at lost people, beggars, criminals, the depraved, and handicapped people in this way focuses on the interference of the devil with God's creation. My friend Corrie ten Boom would never have accepted that perspective and so I replied to my wife, "God does not look at these people and wonder what they could have been. God looks at them and sees them as one day they will be!"

That is indeed a divine perspective. For one day all of creation will be made right. And all who are in Christ will be new creatures.

Jonah needed to see the people of Nineveh not as they were but as what God intended for them to become after He transformed them.

When we see the world this way, looking down from God's perspective, we will no longer see enemies, but people who are lost.

And then we will have the most essential tool for changing the world: compassion!

*Are there people in your life you've given up on, when God is saying
there is still hope? How does your perspective need to change?*

_____

_____

_____

_____

_____

_____

_____

_____

_____

_____

_____

_____

_____

DAY THIRTY-FOUR

⁓

*"But at dawn the next day God provided a worm,
which chewed the vine so that it withered. When the
sun rose, God provided a scorching east wind, and the
sun blazed on Jonah's head so that he grew faint. He
wanted to die, and said, 'It would be better for me to
die than to live.' But God said to Jonah, 'Do you have
a right to be angry about the vine?' 'I do,' he said. 'I am
angry enough to die.'" (Jonah 4:7-9)*

*D*oes Jonah have the right to be angry? He certainly thinks
so. God is making his life miserable. And it won't get any
better when he goes home. Jonah's already worrying that news of his
"treachery" will beat him back to Israel. If they had CNN at that
time, the reporters would be describing a miracle in Nineveh. And
Larry King would be seeking an exclusive interview with Jonah.

Meanwhile King Jeroboam II would be in a rage. He'd be calling
together a tribunal to try Jonah for treason.

So even if Jonah had the right perspective, he couldn't exactly
go home and report the great victory. And if he tried to spiritualize
it—"God made me do it!"—that might make things even worse.

Think about it: Israel has won a great "victory" without firing
a shot. No one died in the process. Not the sailors. Not one of the
Ninevites. The only death recorded in Jonah is of the miracle vine.

Now let me put this in a contemporary context. Suppose, just suppose, that all of Hamas came to be followers of Christ, declared that they would no longer attack Israel, and surrendered their rockets, AK-47s, and suicide bomber belts.

How would the world respond to that news?

Where are the modern-day Jonahs who will go to Hamas, to al Qaeda, to Taliban. To Jedda, to Islamabad, to…?

No one can bring peace who has no peace in his own heart.

Would you rejoice at the news of Hamas, al Qaeda or the Taliban receiving Christ's message? Or would you be angry like Jonah? Why?

DAY THIRTY-FIVE

*"But the LORD said, 'You have been concerned about
this vine, though you did not tend it or make it grow.
It sprang up overnight and died overnight. But Nineveh
has more than a hundred and twenty thousand people
who cannot tell their right hand from their left, and
many cattle as well. Should I not be concerned about
that great city?'" (Jonah 4:10-11).*

*G*od has the final say in the book of Jonah.

Jonah sulks next to the withered remains of a lush vine. The
sun is hot. A scorching east wind buffets him. There is no air conditioning. No comfortable sofa to sit on. And Jonah doesn't like the
drama playing out in front of him, but he can't change the channel.
All he can do is listen to God's voice-over commentary.

Jonah believes he has rights. He has a right to some comfort. He
has a right to that vine even though he didn't plant it or water it or
fertilize it.

God believes the people of Nineveh have rights. They have a
right to know that God is angry with them and has judged their
wicked behavior. They also have a right to know that if they repent,
God offers them grace. Nineveh has a right to know the way of
salvation.

But Nineveh can never know of their rights unless Jonah gives up his right to live his own life in his own way.

So whose rights prevail? Jonah can go to the nursery and select another tree to plant for his shade and comfort. But if the Ninevites don't hear God's message, what hope do they have? They are lost!

It's a matter of perspective, and Jonah definitely has the wrong perspective. So God sets him straight.

I also think God desires for Jonah to *feel* just a little of what God feels for this city. God has compassion for Nineveh. For people who don't know their right hand from their left. Is he talking about the children? Or the mental and physical limitations of Ninevites? Or simply ignorant people? Jonah never asks.

God also has compassion for the animals. They are part of His creation. It was God who told Israel not to muzzle an ox while it is working, which produced Paul's statement, "Is it about oxen that God is concerned?" (I Corinthians 9:9). Jonah, if you don't care for the people, shouldn't you at least care what happens to the animals?

When God stops speaking, Jonah has nothing to say. The book is finished. We are left to wonder about Jonah's reply. Nothing? Is Jonah listening? Is he rebuked and prepared to change his attitude? Or will he sit and continue to pout? Or perhaps he will run away again, turn his back on Nineveh, never pray for them, never follow-up on them to find out if their repentance led to a long-term transformation.

The choice is Jonah's.

The choice is ours.

Today we are left to wonder if we, God's people, will have *any* compassion for a lost world.

If there is compassion in your heart, how is it demonstrated to the world? If there is none, what will it take for you to have compassion on the lost world?

_____

_____

_____

_____

_____

_____

_____

_____

_____

_____

_____

_____

_____

_____

_____

_____

DAY THIRTY-SIX

And Jonah stalked
To his shaded seat
And waited for God
To come around
To his way of thinking.

And God is still waiting
For a host of Jonahs
In their comfortable houses
To come around
To His way of loving.

(*You! Jonah*, by Thomas John Carlisle, Eerdmans, 1968)

Is God waiting on you? How much longer will you make Him wait? How much time do you think you have?

DAY THIRTY-SEVEN

"Nineveh is in ruins—who will mourn for her?"
(Nahum 3:7b)

The story of Nineveh doesn't end with the prophet Jonah. One hundred and thirty years later another prophet preached against this Assyrian city. Nahum's message is the second book after Jonah in the Old Testament. This is the sermon Jonah would love to have preached—from the safety of his own country, certainly not in Nineveh itself.

The message of Nahum is that God's mercy is not unlimited. There is a day of reckoning coming. "The LORD is slow to anger and great in power; the LORD will not leave the guilty unpunished" (Nahum 1:3). Punishment came in 612 B.C. and Nineveh, the great Assyrian city, was destroyed.

Did the people of Nineveh pass the lessons of Jonah on to the next generation? Were they repenting just to save their own necks, or was their's a real heart-change? Given Jonah's attitude, I expect that there was no discipleship, no teaching about the God of the Scriptures, and certainly there was no national reconciliation with Israel. The immediate threat of judgment was removed, but the root causes of Nineveh's wickedness were never addressed.

What Nineveh experienced was God's grace. They had a wake-up call, but then they hit the snooze button and went back to sleep.

God put the responsibility on the leadership. "O king of Assyria, your shepherds slumber; your nobles lie down to rest. Your people are scattered on the mountains with no one to gather them" (Nahum 3:18).

The messages of Jonah and Nahum causes me to think of another alarming lesson. In times of peace and prosperity, we may be in greater danger. Sometimes persecution or affliction keeps us alert. The media noticed that after the September 11 attacks on America, the following Sunday churches were packed. One month later, attendance had returned to normal. It was the same in my country when Germany invaded Holland; at the end of World War II all those people stopped coming to church.

So what do Jonah and Nahum teach us?

Like Nineveh, the Muslim world today has not received the offer of God's grace.

Will we jump immediately to Nahum's message of judgment?
Will we hear the call of Jonah—but run away?
Or will we hear God's call and respond with compassion? How can we not offer Muslims God's Amazing Grace package?

DAY THIRTY-EIGHT

"A wicked and adulterous generation looks for a miraculous sign, but none will be given it except the sign of Jonah.' Jesus then left them and went away" (Matthew 16:4).

"For as Jonah was three days and three nights in the belly of a huge fish, so the Son of Man will be three days and three nights in the heart of the earth. The men of Nineveh will stand up at the judgment with this generation and condemn it; for they repented at the preaching of Jonah, and now one greater than Jonah is here" (Matthew 12:40-41).

"As the crowds increased, Jesus said, 'This is a wicked generation. It asks for a miraculous sign, but none will be given it except the sign of Jonah. For as Jonah was a sign to the Ninevites, so also will the Son of Man be to this generation" (Luke 11:29-30).

Jonah "died" and was buried in the belly of a fish. Was it the end? No. Three days later he rose again and offered new life to Nineveh.

Jesus died and was buried. Was it the end? No! Three days later he rose from the dead.

We can never make too much of that historic event. It is the reason for our existence. "I know that my Redeemer liveth!" Let's go and proclaim it! That's what Peter did on the day of Pentecost. He declared how Jesus was put to death on a cross. "But God raised him from the dead, freeing him from the agony of death, because it was impossible for death to keep its hold on him" (Acts 2:24).

The early church lived as if Jesus died yesterday.

The early church lived as if Jesus rose today.

The early church lived as if Jesus would return tomorrow.

That's a great way to live in the twenty first century!

So what is our business? Peter explains: "In your hearts set apart Christ as Lord. Always be prepared to give an answer to everyone who asks you to give the reason for the hope that you have" (I Peter 3:15). Always. The world wants to know, *needs* to know, how they can be saved. How their sins can be forgiven. How they can go to Heaven when they die.

Nineveh did not know.

The sailors did not know.

But Jonah knew.

So together let's make a radical decision—don't let the world die in ignorance of the gospel.

Are you prepared to give the world an answer to the question "How can we be saved?" How can you live life today as if Jesus will return tomorrow?

_____

_____

_____

_____

_____

_____

_____

_____

_____

_____

_____

_____

_____

_____

_____

_____

DAY THIRTY-NINE

"No one cares for my life" (Psalm 142:4b).

$\mathcal{I}$ wonder, is this the source of terrorism?

There are people who have never known the Kingdom of God. They are totally stripped of every shred of worth, except perhaps from their immediate family...and their terrorist cell. They may be religious. They may pray five times a day and follow rigid religious rules. But has anyone ever stood in front of them, looked in their eyes and shared the love of Jesus with them?

This is the heart of God. And we can only have it when we *know* God.

Since no one volunteered to go to Nineveh, God conscripted the only prophet He had available. Jonah was obedient, ultimately and reluctantly, but he got no personal benefit, no credit for the miracle in Nineveh, because of the hardness of his heart. He refused to understand God's compassion.

Hopefully God has more volunteers today. Perhaps you now have a desire to go to Muslims. But how? You had better know God before you run off to try and do His work. And you'd better know God's message before you go and witness to your neighbor.

Where do we begin? Clearly we must begin with prayer. When you see bad news on television, do you immediately connect that bad news to the heart of God? How does He view that situation? Closer to home, do you pray for the people in your neighborhood? For the Muslims you see in your supermarket? Have you prayed for the people who attend the mosque in your city? Have you considered visiting that mosque? Maybe you should invite the imam over for coffee and become his friend.

Do you have a burden for a Muslim country? Then pray! Soon you will probably cry for that country. Jesus was moved with compassion for the people, because they were like sheep without a shepherd. We must pray first, and seek to know God's heart, and then we will have love and compassion. Then we can listen for and receive God's message. Then we can hear the call of God for a place or a people. He will then provide the direction, plus the means to go, including the gifts, the funds and all the resources we need.

We are to be witnesses and not judges.

We are to be servants and not superiors.

We are to respect and not despise.

That is the Christian life.

What is the number one message you have gained from this study of Jonah?

How is God challenging you to respond to His call to seek and save the LOST?

Who does God want you to pray for? A person? A country? When will you begin?

_____

_____

_____

_____

_____

_____

_____

_____

_____

_____

_____

_____

_____

_____

_____

_____

_____

_____

_____

_____

GET INVOLVED!

Open Doors started in 1955 when a Dutch missionary discovered that Christians in Communist countries were desperately longing for Bibles and supplies – and so he began to take Christian literature behind the Iron Curtain. He became known as Brother Andrew – 'God's Smuggler' – and the founder of a ministry still rooted in a passion to follow God's call and release His Word into the lives of believers in the world's most difficult areas.

More than fifty years later Open Doors continues to serve persecuted Christians in around fifty countries, whether the oppression comes in the name of Communism, Buddhism, Hinduism or Islam. Where the people of God are under pressure, Open Doors stands with them, responding to their cries for help and shaping its response under their guidance.

Prayerful involvement with Open Doors is a great way to strengthen the Persecuted Church, not just to face the onslaught of pressure, but to continue to reach out with the Gospel of Jesus Christ.

Right now Open Doors is ready to give you information for your prayers – the authentic voice of the Persecuted Church brought to you in print, by email, and on the web, so that your prayers are timely, informed and effective weapons in the spiritual battle.

Right now Open Doors can channel your gifts to where they will make a significant difference to our sisters and brothers in the Persecuted Church, not least in providing the Bibles and other Christian literature they have requested. You will be helping to train pastors and congregations so that they can stand strong through the storm, to strengthen the Church in its commitment to mission, to make sure that those who have lost so much can receive material help and spiritual encouragement.

Many Christians around the world also volunteer to bring the Persecuted Church into the life of their own church family, sharing news for prayer and exploring the lessons to be learned from our sisters and brothers.

Perhaps you would allow Open Doors to become your link to the Persecuted Church, so that together we can all play our part in God's great plan and purpose for His world. For further information, simply contact the national office listed on the next page—and discover more of the miracles that come with obedience to God's call.

Open Doors AUSTRALIA
PO Box 6237
French Forest NSW 2086
www.opendoors.org.au
Email: ODAustralia@od.org

Open Doors CANADA
30-5155 Spectrum Way
Mississauga, ON
L4W 5A1
www.opendoorsca.org
Email: OpenDoorsCA@od.org

Open Doors NEW ZEALAND
PO Box 27630
Mt Roskill
Auckland 1440
www.OpenDoors.org.nz
Email: OpenDoorsNZ@od.org

Open Doors SOUTH AFRICA
PO Box 1771
Cresta
2118
www.OpenDoors.org.za
Email: SouthAfrica@od.org

Open Doors USA
P0 Box 27001
Santa Ana, CA 92799
www.OpenDoorsUSA.org
Email: USA@OpenDoors.org

For information on Open Doors offices worldwide
please see www.OpenDoors.org.

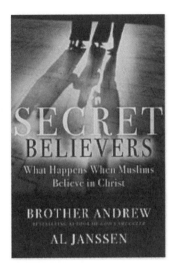

In his most incredible and eye-opening book to date, Brother Andrew invites you to meet brave men and women you never knew existed. This is the riveting true story of the church in Islamic countries struggling to come to grips with hostile governments, terrorist acts, and an influx of Muslims coming to Christ. The names and places have been changed to protect the real people in real places. But the stories are true.

Secret Believers not only gives you a glimpse of the lives of these courageous believers, it also proposes four practical initiatives for Christians in the West to help these persecuted brothers and sisters. It calls us to join a new kind of jihad, leaving vengeance behind in favor of forgiveness, radical love, and unyielding prayer.

"Brother Andrew and Al Janssen reveal the amazing stories of those who witness the love of One they once refused and passionately searched until they found Him, even in the face of great opposition. Theirs is a testament to meekness, grace, and triumph, and a call to every follower of Christ to mirror their example."

–RAVI ZACHARIAS, author and speaker

"The Book of Acts is filled with prayer meetings; every forward thrust the first church made was immersed in prayer. Take another look at the church at Pentecost. They prayed ten days and preached ten minutes and three thousand people were saved. Today we pray ten minutes and preach ten days and are ecstatic if anyone is saved."

—RONALD DUNN

. . .

Brother Andrew and Al Janssen recount their journey of praying for 22 men in Muslim countries, all potential pastors. "Within six months, two of these brothers had died a martyr's death." The personal crisis that followed led both men to a powerful, deeper understanding of prayer—one they want to share with you. This powerful booklet can be used as a tool for personal or group study. The "Take Action" steps are provided at the end of each chapter in hopes of challenging you to take your prayer life to a new and deeper level.

God invites us to influence our community, our nation and the world—to literally direct history while we're on our knees... The course of an entire nation could be changed by one person saying to God, "What then will you do for your great name?"